W9-DGL-083

The Joy of Christmas

The Joy of Christmas

Gifts of
the Human
and Divine

Daniel C. Price, Ph.D.

Printed in the United States of America

ISBN
0-9664464-0-2

Published by:
Price Publications LLC
1004 W. Michigan Avenue
Jackson, Michigan 49202

Web Address: www.pricepublications.com

Oh, to Know
The Joy of Christmas

To know the joy of Christmas is to know the gifts within gifts, the gifts of this world within the gifts of worlds beyond this world.

Acknowledgements

Thank you, thank you, thank you... to the Angelic Presence, to family, and to friends, all of whom are a part of this book, for your wisdom, guidance, support, encouragement, and gifts of wonder.

Artwork by Connie Price and Sarah Price
Editing by Jackie Minkel, Connie and Sarah Price

Graphic Design by Frog Productions

The Joy of Christmas

Gifts of the Human and Divine

by Daniel C. Price, Ph.D.

In 1991 I had an amazing experience that changed my life. While driving in my car I felt a presence. This was followed by a series of wonderful metaphysical insights about Santa Claus, the Christmas tree, and the evergreen wreath. Since then Christmas has never been the same for me.

Because of this new awareness, my life feels richer and I more Spiritual. "The Joy of Christmas" is my way of sharing this experience with others, and I hope these insights also serve to help you enrich your life... and your Spirituality.

To Oneness...

Contents

This is a book of Christmas metaphors... a metaphor is a figure of speech where one kind of object or idea is used in place of another to suggest a likeness between them. For example, the metaphor of Santa Claus is used to suggest the likeness of God.

Finding the meaning in these metaphors creates a new level of awareness and expands our joy so we can enjoy both the human and Spiritual as One. And sometimes new awareness comes to us in the most unusual way...

The Spiritual Ride

Last minute
shopping
late
getting
home
I feel
slight
distress
must
press
ahead
the trunk
of
my car
slightly
ajar
packed
with
presents
for
Christmas

I want
to be
home
to
the joy
and
warmth
of
Christmas Eve

hence . . .

the
need
to speed
but
indeed
the
risks
are
great

Snow flakes
glittering
in the
half-light
hinder
sight
run
straight
into
my windshield

and
hitting

faster
than
the wipers
can
clear
create
fear . . .

This
    snow
that
    I've
    watched
            grow
to
a menacing
            size
    is
        driven
    by
        a cold
            biting
                uninviting
                    wind

Heater
    on high
        defrost
            blasting
I squint
    to see
        the road

a road
    covered
        in
    white
            drifts

                and
                    glaring
                        ice

Accelerating
doesn't
help
when
tires
lose
traction

The
sudden
sliding
action
feels
like
a magnet's
attraction
for

snow banks

I must
get home
safe
and
sound
and
I
picture
the
family
gathering
'round
for
dinner

It's lonely
in my
car
though
I haven't
gone
far
when
I sense
a vague
presence

and now
somehow
I know

I am
not
alone . . .

What could
this
be?

What is happening to me?

A daydream
winter storm
delusion
or
just utter
confusion

My mind
paces
races
past reason

but

how
strange

whatever
it is
I feel
close
comfort

This presence
is
unclear
perhaps
just
my
fear
or
could
it be
an
extension
of me . . .

merely . . .

my shadow?

Eyes
blinking
mood
sinking
I
cannot
bring it
into
clear
focus
not
to
mention
trying
to pay
attention
to the road

I
sense it

and feel
what I
cannot see

I know
something
is next
to me. . .

Feels like
a misty
somewhat
twisty
shape
with long
soft
arms
more
like

feathers

wings

Now,
now
I sense
with greater
clarity
this
rarity

What
started
as
an
inner
knowing
is
now
someone
showing
herself
to me

Now
now suddenly
she
is
clearer
nearer
an
energy
like you
or
me

could it be . . .

next
to me . . .

an **Angel!**

Frightened . . .

I shake
my head
to
be sure
I'm not
misled
or perhaps
even
dead

I
sense
no harm
so there's
less
cause
for alarm
as I drive
in my car
with

an Angel

not far

away

Hard to
believe
or even
conceive
of this
happening
but
I now
begin
to feel
a real
peace

I see
what
mesmerizes
me

a warmth
an
understanding
commanding
my
attention . . .

The Angel Speaks

She starts
to speak
rather
slowly
at first

You wonder
why
I'm here . . .

No need
to fear
please
just hear
a truth
I want
to make
clear

Just relax
and watch
the road

You can
still drive
and
listen

If my
ideas
seem
new
the purpose
is to
enlighten

not frighten

you

Christmas
offers
the joy
of gifts
within gifts

two gifts
in each one

That's
the fun
of seeing
how
both sides
of one coin
join
together

This may
sound new
but not
surprise you

Gifts can be
enjoyed
on two
levels
at the same
time
and thus
combine
the human

and Divine

Age-old
traditions
at first
conceal
then
reveal
through
each
metaphor
new worlds
to
explore

I am
intrigued
by
her words
and
through
my
silence
have agreed
to
at least
listen

With a loving
grin
she starts
right in . . .

Christmas
celebrates
the ***birth***
of a new
awareness
when
the ***ultimate***
Love
given
from heaven
above
is brought
to earth
a
demonstration
of each
human's
worth

Now
hold tight
for
the next
delight . . .

Santa Claus

Thoughtfully
she shares
with me...

Because
Spirit
you
cannot
see
the image
of Santa
needs
to be

Though
it may seem
rather odd

Santa Claus
is . . .

at his
core
a metaphor

the ***unseen***
Loving
Being

Now think!

If you
had
your
druthers
how would
you
show
God
to others?

In human
terms
what size
shape
would
He / She be?

What
colors
would you
want
to see?

If God
is
the essence
of the
Universe
without
beginning
and
without
end

as far
as humans
can see

He must be...

very
very
old

God's age
and wisdom
can be seen
in Santa's
long
white
beard

Dressed
in a suit
of
red
trimmed
in
white
it's a great
delight
to know
that
your
subconscious
has
gotten
it right!

Human beings . . .

as they
grow
old
have features that
change

As time
and genetics
re
arrange
bodies
become more
round
as they
put on
that
extra
pound

Hair
turns color
too
as youth
does not
stay
and
older age
brings on
gray

When
very old
much
to their
delight
if
they keep
their hair
it changes
to white

So
colors
have meaning
too
though
this is nothing new

Red
can be said
to have
many
meanings

Anger
is thought of
as red
especially
when blood
is shed
but
the opposite
is also
true
when
a valentine
is sent
to you

Now picture
the color
of a loving
heart
and you
will start
to see
that
universally
red
is said
to be
the color
of
Love

Now
can you
see
how easy
this can
be?

Santa
represents
the best
as he
is dressed
in God's
qualities

Surely
you can
see
by his suit
of red
and white
and
with such
a beautiful
beard
he
is not
to be feared
but
seen as
an Eternal
Being
of warmth
and
wisdom
and
Pure
Love

Santa is
the human
connection
a reflection
of affection
from heaven
above
of ***heavenly***
Love

Dressed
in red
and
white
Santa
represents
God's
Love
and
Light!

Santa
appears
from above
and represents
the highest
thoughts
the ***highest***
Love
if you want proof
just look up . . .

look on

the roof!

That is where
his sleigh
will stay
while he,
in a way
you cannot
see,
will enter
your loving
center

But
when you
are living
with stress
I would guess
it is hard
to feel
your special ness

When living
with hurt
and anger
trying to survive

how could
such
a Great Love
arrive?

Because this is hard
to conceive
or even
believe
this magical event
heaven sent
is shown
to you
in a way
you can see . . .

He comes

down
your
chimney!

The chimney
is the
channel

a clever way
to portray
in a picture
how the highest Love
comes down to earth
and is given
birth
in your heart

Try to see
Spiritually

What does God do?

How does
God
come
to you?

To help you see
how this can be
Santa
slides down
your chimney
and lands
with such grace
in your fireplace

His landing
is your heart
expanding

And while you
lay sleeping
unaware
that he is
there
his promise
he is keeping

After landing with
a rather quiet
ka-boom
he goes right
to work
in your
"living room"

His gifts
are left
for you to find
inside

Now
he
has complied
with your
greatest wish

Rather
than
leaving you
apart
God's Love
lives
in your ***heart***

I
just wish
you
knew
how
this
Special
Love
is
within
each
of
you!

Christmas Stockings

Then
the Angel
went on
to say

Please
remember
what
you learn
today

God
is
a special
kind of Love

Most humans
live
with great
suspicion
but
God's Love
is given
without
condition

And
I think
it's fair
to say
that
on earth
though
you certainly
care

Pure Love

is very
very
rare

Because
human life
is filled
with struggle
and strife
people
pray
for understanding

Minds burn
hearts yearn
for such
a gift

This Loving
understanding
must
come to earth
from a higher
view
in order to
help you
re-new

Imagine
how you
might create
relate
through
an image
a human's need
to be filled
with higher
understanding

Though
this insight
may seem
shocking
picture
the
Christmas Stocking

Now
this part
is really
neat
mentally
the feet
on which
you stand
take command
are your
beliefs

Just like
stockings
are made
displayed
in the shape
of your feet

your understanding
shapes
your beliefs

This just
goes to show
how important
understanding *is!*

So
empty stockings
are hung
with care
right where
Santa
comes in
hoping
He
will soon
be there
and
fill
your
understanding

And if
God's Love
was really
understood
it would
change
your world!

Christmas Presents

Christmas is
sharing
showing
caring

This tradition
of giving
is what you
have been
living

To feel deeply
content
understand
what ***gifts***
represent

God resorts
to all
sorts
of wrappings

For a quick critique
try to see
how unique
you all are

Now imagine
opening a present
on
Christmas Day

In the same way
when you ***look***
within *yourself*
you begin
to see
the surprise
and how
wise
to look ***with***
new eyes

Deep within
yourself
your gift
can be seen . . .

the **endless Love**
that you are
inside
a human being!

In order
to see
your gift
of Spirit
to really
hear it
it helps
to raise
your awareness
higher

This is often hard
for you to do

When fear
and pain
sustain
separation
they pull you
away

That is when
it is hard
to ***stay***
centered

I have noticed
how people
on earth
sep ar ate
often
do not relate
things
to one another
to one
and
the other

For instance
they
try to decide
if Christmas
is a celebration
of Spiritual
elation
or
economic
creation

But all gifts
and money spent
are expressions
of heaven sent
creativity

So
the physical
that you see
is one side
of Spirituality

Two in One
that is the fun
of it

Looking at
Christmas
with enlightened
eyes
you will see
in all the
creativity
the specialness
of the presents
is . . .

the ***Presence!***

Love . . .
Free Will . . .
Your Soul's Mission

God's Love
is given
as gifts
of endless
creativity

Just look around
what else do you see
but more
and more
variety

In fact
so that
the gift
of creativity
is not misconstrued
try to see
God
in the multitude

Since such Love
is within
each of you
it is only natural
to express
what is true . . .

the Love
within you

Giving Love
creates
Love

Now imagine
how creative
you would have to
be
to think
in terms
of life
and Love
Eternally

The human side
is limited
but the

Spirit

lives on
and

The One
is in each
side
of the other
which
is another
Christmas gift

The Angel
leans
nearer
her tone
clearer

The
ultimate
gifts
like
a covenant
to fulfill

include
life
itself
and
free will

It's
this gift
this very
gift
of ***free will***
that lets
one
sift
through
life's
experiences

With
this gift
yes!
this gift!
this
very gift . . .

with the gift
of
free will

your soul's
mission
you can
fulfill!

Through
experiences
in life
through
pain
and
strife
you learn
to make
choices

You are
free
as you
can see
each day
to stay
or
turn away

But
try
to be
knowingly
like
the elf
who
works
for
Santa Claus
to
fulfill
His great
cause

And like
the elf
serve
your highest
Spiritual
Self

Can you start
to see
what she
is telling
me?

This Angel
who is
quite
clever
understands
that we
often
sever
our
ties
to our
higher
Loving
Self

Our
Spiritual side
can remain
hidden
when
one
feels
forbidden
to peek
or
even
seek
greater
meaning

She urges
us
as you might
suspect
to **re---connect**
with our
Loving
Self

I start
to comprehend
this Spiritual
friend

As her words
flow
through
my mind
I realize
God's gift
of
Love

is ours
to find!

Her words
touch me
deeply
and
I can
feel
tears
welling up
in
my
eyes

My body
begins
to tremble
as my
thoughts
reassemble

A feeling
of
electricity
cascades
down
my spine

I try
to pretend
defend
against
deep
feelings
stay cool
calm
but
skin
is thin
mine
quivers
shivers

My mind
stretches
to remain
sane
while I
entertain

amazing

possibilities . . .

She is
opening my eyes
but the
next
metaphor
is a complete
surprise

She wants
me
to really see . . .

the
Christmas Tree

and

once again

she stretches
my attention
not to
mention
my

understanding . . .

Evergreen . . .
Eternal Being

She looks
as though
she can
see
straight
through
me

Eyes
dancing
with delight
spirit
taking
flight
laughing
with
glee
she brightens

enlightens. . .

questions
me
about
this tree
about
what
can be
seen
like
the fact
that
it's
an
evergreen!

With twinkling eyes
she continues
her surprise

Think!

What
does it
show
what
do you
know
about
this
special
tree?

The color
green
can be
seen
as the color
of
growth
and
of
life

Think!

The word
ever
implies

never
ending!

Ever green . . .

always giving
always living

The mystery
unravels
travels
on words
that reveal
what
needs
to be
seen
the Eternal
aspects
of ***your***

Spiritual
Being

A mystery
revealed
in the name
alone!
It's
a great
insight
I'm being
shown

I adore
this
metaphor
of
the
evergreen

What
a
clever
way
to
display

Eternal
Life

This
Spiritual
gift
extends
beyond
earthly
life
beyond
earthly
strife
beyond
the
infernal
into
the
Eternal!

From
this life
into. . .

the next

the next
context

That's
the gift. . .

the invention
of
ascension

the
everlasting
life
of
the **soul!**

How clever!

This gift
lasts
forever!

My mind
ricochets
between
her
ideas
and my
previous
understanding

Now
I see
the symbol
of this
tree
and
her views
I can
use
to enjoy
Christmas
more

to enjoy
Christmas
as never
before . . .

Christmas Light

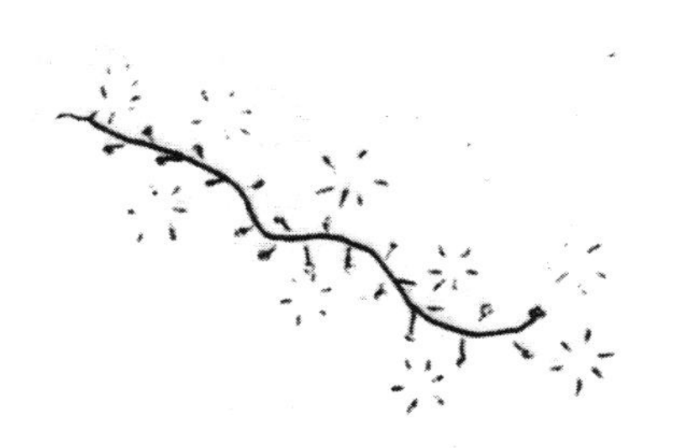

My Angel my
new found
friend

asks me
to pretend

Let's continue
this
journey
you and me
around
the
Tree
of
Eternity

Think Spiritually!

What
do they
mean
those lights
so bright?

What is
the glowing
insight. . .

of the
ornamentation
colorful
decoration?

On earth
people
decorate
one
another
to express
recognition
that
some
special
ambition
or
condition
has been
achieved

With your
insistence
I'll
provide
a
for
instance . . .

A soldier
is decorated
with a
medal
for
great valor
and
Santa's elves
would
certainly
grin
if
decorated
with a
pin

Yes!
decorated
because
they
help
by
filling
a stocking
or making
a rocking
horse

gifts and toys
for
girls
and
boys

What
I am
trying
to say
is that
in the same way
people
decorate
their
Christmas Tree

Remember
those
candy canes
you bought
each
a sweet thought
hanging
on the Tree
of Eternity

Stripes
of red and white
signify
Spirit's
Eternal
Love** and **Light

As people see
more openly
they see Love
as Eternity
they see
Love and Light
in you
and me
in
all
of God's
creativity

How do you
display
such an array
of enlightenment?

At first people
lit
small candles
fastened them to
the evergreen tree
showing
subconsciously
that they ***see***

the ***Eternity***
of Spirit

As consciousness
increases
and darkness
ceases
more lights
are displayed

Look around
and you can
see
how beautiful
understanding
can be!

Lights on trees
inside
the house
and out
without a doubt
shine
like
Divine
Illumination!

Guiding Light

Ah, yes!
I picture
the scene
of Christmas
and
the evergreen
full of
light

red

green

and
white

Squinting
through
eyelashes
fills
the room
with splashes
of colored
light

I remember
the warmth
of that
light
seen
on a
cold
frosty
night

Breaking
into
my reverie
she
says
to me
with more
than a little curiosity

Do you see how dark
it is outside
how hard it is
to see?

This is why people
live
in such dread

inside
their head
*is **darkness***
too . . .

Goodness knows
when the wind
of bitterness
blows
a chill
can fill
your heart

This is
winter's dark
and
dreary
side
the weary side
of you

When the reality
of
Spirituality
is frozen
in disbelief
and negativity snows
you in
this is
when
you are indeed
in need
of **Light**

And so
placed
at the top
of the
tree
is the
Angel

which,
come
to think
of it,
looks
a lot
like
me!

The Angel
represents
an aspect
of
heaven
a reflection
of
God's
affection

Angels
are links
between
heaven
and
earth

and unless
you
decide
to hide
from your
higher
Self
your Angel
is here
as a
guide
to
show you
your
Spiritual
side

The connection
between
heaven
and
earth
this crowning
glory
tells
its
own
story

A star
or
an Angel
whose
light

guides
you
through
the
darkness
of
night

guides you
to the
Christ
Light

This light
of ***Love***
that illumines
you
and
me
guides us
shining
through
Eternity

Now
you can
see
why you
light up
the
Christmas Tree . . .

Never Alone

Suddenly
the car
starts
to go
into
a slide

what a ride

and
I am filled
with
a chilling
fear
I cannot
hide

On ice
hidden
below
the snow
tires
lose
their
traction
and the weight
of the
car
carries us
far

Blinded
by this snow
I cannot
see
where
the slide is
carrying
me . . .

Muscles
tighten
hands
grip
the wheel
but
I cannot
feel
the road

If I
cannot
steer
how can
I
stay clear
of danger?

Pump
the breaks

hold the line

catch
my
breath
and
pray
I'll be
fine . . .

Finally,
now from
***deep* inside**
my fear
begins
to
subside

A calm
washes
over me
and somehow
I see

that
I am
never
alone

It is
    hard
to describe
    and
            I wonder
    if
    I've
        lied
to
    myself

As
I relax
I hear
her explain...

Most people
struggle
as
you
can see
because
the
five senses
that detect
and
connect
with
the
physical world
sight
sound
smell
taste
and touch
all reveal
much
but also

limit
awareness

Though
your senses
work
wonderfully
well
for living
in
the physical
dimension
they also
create
a
suspension
of higher
awareness

It's true
and I
need
to
comprehend
that I
am a
blend

I have
a human
side
that I
hold dear
but
it is
often
full
of
fear

The other side
which
I can now better
perceive
at times
has been
hard to
believe

the side
I had
not
been
seeing...

the helping
hand
of my
Spiritual
Being!

As I re---connect
with
my
Spiritual
center

deep breaths
frost
the windshield
and I
yield
my
tension
away

What
a **gift**
this
shift
in
perception
provides!

The Angel's
warmth
I sense
and now
with
renewed
confidence
we
laugh
together
traveling
through
thick
wet
cold
weather. . .

Oneness

In her own
angelic way
my Angel
goes on
to
say...

If
the material
world
you
perceive
is all
in which
you
believe
then you miss

the truth

You are

a ***synergy***
of
Spiritual
energy!

These
two systems
the ***human***
and ***Divine***
intertwine
and
combine
to form
a greater
reality
than just
what
human eyes
can see

Please
don't be
offended
but
your ***limits***
can be
transcended
by looking
beyond
the
obvious

One of
the simplest
forms
of Christmas
decoration
is also
cause
for
great
adoration
most
beautiful
to
behold
and in meaning
I am told
most
Spiritual

Imagine
what
could be seen
what
it could mean
a
wreath
of deep
evergreen

This circle
is a
visual
communion
a **re-union**

It is
the ***journey***
of life
like
Christ's
from
Spirit
into
human
form
then

from
this life
after
such strife
to the
next
life
from
this world
swirled
into
the next
world
then
from there
to
here
and back
to Spirit
once
again

His
path
wound
round
like
the wreath

and
took him
full
circle

This is
your path
too
something your soul
already knew

Living in a world
of
sep ar ation
is preparation
for the
return to
Oneness

The wreath
shows how
separate
branches now
come
together

sep ar ate
yet
One

It's a fine
line
this intertwine
of human
and
Divine
one into
the
other
all
aspects
of One
another

Please
believe me
try to see
what seems far
is near

There . . .

is also
here!

The Christmas Wreath
signifies
dignifies
the ***Oneness***
of Spirit
with
mankind

This awareness
of **One**
is a lot
of fun

As you
believe
so too
you can
achieve

Just
open
your
consciousness
and
in a
phenomenal
way
you can
celebrate
Christmas
every day!

These Gifts

This gift
of Christmas
Love
is a part
of
human life
and
the gift
of life
as you
now
can see
is
everlasting
Love
*and **life***
Eternally

Now consider
the joy
of your
awareness
which
in all
fairness
is another
Christmas
gift

Remember
she says
though
I
cannot
stay
and
as she speaks
begins
to fade
away

what we have shared
on this snowy
day
will help you
enjoy life
along the way

Each ***truth***
please remember
is like
a
glowing
growing
ember
meant to warm
and take form
within you

I know
she needs
to go
and
I miss her
already
so
I must
steady
myself

It has been
such
a relief
to widen
my belief

to know
that what is
right
in front
of me
humanly
is also
an opportunity
to see
Spirituality

I can't
wait
to get
home

I want
to look
once
again
at
our
Christmas
Tree

I want
to see
beyond
the tree
and
see life
as Eternity

I now can
see
each
metaphor
and
open
my mind's
door

I want
to appreciate
even more
the gifts
we give
the life
we live

for now
I can
really
understand
what deep
meaning
it all
holds
for
me

I know now
how
the gift
of
understanding
is the gift
you
give
yourself

I am
in awe
of how
our
subconscious
knows
and shows
us
proof
of truth
and of
the joy
in store
in each
metaphor

I know we
decorate
a
tree
symbolically
and
I can see
how red and white
show
God's
Love and **Light**

And how
Love
is the great
cause
behind
Santa Claus

I now
see
beneath
the surface
of
the wreath
how
the **human**
and **Divine**

intertwine

This is
such a **joy**
to
be enlightened
rather
than live
so frightened
not knowing
not growing

I know
I have journeyed
far
by car
and I am growing
in my knowing
guided
by the **light**
of **insight**

and
in my
estimation
I've
arrived
at a
new
destination

And so
my Angel
I am
forever
grateful
to have met
in such
a wonderfully
fateful
way
and in my heart
you will
stay
for the
rest
of my days

and
for always

I can
still feel
she is near
though
her voice
is a mere
whisper . . .

Remember
the warm ember
inside
use it
as a guide
and
do not
hide

your ***Love***

Christmas is
a gift
of
Joy

a gift
of
Hope

a gift
of
Love

And you know
this gift
from
above
this
Love
is
by far
what
you really are!

Merry
Christmas!

To order The Joy of Christmas
www.pricepublications.com
US $14.95
CAN $21.00